Pat the Pets

Written by
Stephen Rickard

The dog is a bit sad.
I can pat the dog.

If I pat the dog, it is not sad.
The dog can run in the sun.

The cat in the hat is a bit sad.
I can pat the cat in the hat.

If I pat the cat in the hat,
it is not sad.

The cat in the hat
can sit in the sun.

A duck is not a pet.

The duck is a bit sad.
I can pat the duck.

If I pat the duck, it is not sad.

The duck can run in the sun.

The rat in a sock is a bit sad.
I can pat the rat in a sock.

If I pat the rat in a sock,
it is not sad.

The rat in a sock
can sit in the sun.

A pig is not a pet.

The pig is a bit sad.
I can pat the pig.

If I pat the pig,
it is not sad.

The pig can sit
in the sun.

Can I pat a bat?

A bat is not a pet.

I can pat a bat, but a bat cannot run in the sun!